FENIX
INNOVATION

ADRIANA LUNA CARLOS
Editor-In-Chief, Designer
and Co-Founder

HANNA OLIVAS
Managing Editor &
Co-Founder

NICOLE CURTIS
Director of the SRS
Magazine Division

ADVERTISING OPPORTUNITIES
Info@SheRisesStudios.com

FENIX INNOVATION
APRIL 2025

SHE RISES
STUDIOS

CONTACT US
SheRisesStudios@gmail.com

WWW.SHERISESSTUDIOS.COM

LETTER FROM THE EDITORS

Dear Reader,

Welcome to the April 2025 edition of FENIX Innovation Magazine, where we celebrate the pioneers redefining tomorrow's digital landscape. This issue, *BUILDING THE FUTURE: App Development In The Digital Age,* spotlights the visionaries shaping mobile experiences, blending creativity with cutting-edge technology.

We are thrilled to feature Jewels Lamm on this month's cover. As the founder of InBody: Rewire For Love and Connection, Jewels brings a unique perspective on leadership and transformation. Her work, rooted in somatic practices and nervous system regulation, demonstrates that innovation isn't just about technology—it's also about human connection, self-awareness, and breaking free from limiting cycles.

Throughout this edition, you'll discover insights into the future of app development, creative digital solutions, and stories from trailblazers driving innovation. From emerging trends in streaming and gaming to the artistry behind mobile content, this issue offers a glimpse into the future of digital media.

At FENIX, we remain committed to unveiling the innovators, creators, and changemakers who inspire us all to embrace bold ideas and reimagine what's possible.

Warm regards,

Adriana Luna Carlos and Hanna Olivas
Editors of FENIX Innovation Magazine

FENIX TV

SHE RISES STUDIOS

she wins

NICE GIRLS FINISH FIRST

SHE WINS
VIRTUAL SUMMIT 2025

When: May 14–16, 2025
Where: Exclusively on FENIX TV
Tickets: $49.97

Join us for the **She Wins Virtual Summit 2025**, a 3-day event celebrating women entrepreneurs and leaders from around the world. This year's theme, **"Nice Girls Finish First,"** showcases how kindness, empathy, and integrity drive success in business and life.

What to Expect:

- Inspiring stories from women leaders.
- Expert advice on leadership, resilience, and growth.
- Strategies for thriving in business without compromising values.

BE PART OF THIS EMPOWERING MOVEMENT AND DISCOVER HOW KINDNESS LEADS TO GREATNESS!

WWW.SHERISESSTUDIOS.COM/SHEWINSVIRTUALSUMMIT2025

Jewels Lamm is the visionary founder of InBody: Rewire For Love and Connection, a transformational coaching practice designed to help women break free from cycles of perfectionism, control, and judgment. Through her work, Jewels facilitates a healing journey of the heart, guiding ambitious women and leaders toward deep self-love, joy, and success. Her signature Restore Love Within 1:1 coaching program is a testament to her belief that true success comes from within, where women learn to embody their most radiant selves.

With a background spanning 20 years as a creative entrepreneur —from owning a restaurant franchise to becoming a wellness coach—Jewels understands firsthand that entrepreneurship is a deeply spiritual journey. She believes that success should not come at the cost of well-being and that loving oneself is the key to thriving in both business and life. Based in Cincinnati, Ohio, she offers complimentary Get Unstuck sessions via Zoom, empowering women worldwide to step into their fullest potential.

The Birth of InBody: Rewire For Love and Connection
Jewels' journey to founding InBody was deeply personal. Outwardly, she appeared to have it all—success, ambition, and control over her life. Yet internally, she felt unfulfilled and disconnected.

REWIRING FOR SUCCESS:

Jewels Lamm on the Intersection of Mindset, Nervous System, & Leadership

She continuously pushed herself, believing that the next milestone would bring her the wholeness she longed for. However, no achievement could quiet the underlying sense of not being enough.

Over time, her body began sending unmistakable signals—tension, exhaustion, and anxiety—forcing her to listen. It was then that she realized she had been living in her head, disconnected from her body's wisdom. Her true healing began when she stopped chasing worth through accomplishments and started rewiring her nervous system to feel safe in simply being. Now, through InBody, she helps high-achieving women break free from overdoing, overthinking, and overcontrolling so they can experience love, connection, and joy from within.

Breaking Free from Perfectionism and Control

Many ambitious women find themselves trapped in cycles of control and perfectionism. They do the mindset work, affirmations, and gratitude practices, yet something still feels missing. They operate from their minds, analyzing and planning, but remain disconnected from their bodies.

Jewels has identified a hidden fear that drives this pattern: "If I slow down, I will fall apart. If I'm not achieving, I am not worthy." Through her coaching, she helps clients move beyond intellectual understanding and into a body-based transformation. Utilizing somatic processing, she guides women to uncover and release suppressed emotions, shifting from a mindset of proving their worth to feeling their inherent value.

The Restore Love Within 1:1 Coaching Program

Jewels' signature program, Restore Love Within, offers a personalized experience tailored to each woman's nervous system, emotional patterns, and healing journey. Unlike a one-size-fits-all approach, this program works by harnessing the body's intelligence to foster deep emotional healing.

The program is designed for ambitious women who have done the inner work yet still feel stuck. They are exhausted from constantly pushing and proving themselves and are ready to return home to themselves. Through this transformative process, clients shift from fear and contraction to trust, expansion and self-love.

The Role of Somatic and Nervous System Regulation in Healing

True healing goes beyond mindset shifts; it is a felt experience within the body. Many women intellectually understand what they need to do but struggle to embody that knowledge. Stress, emotional wounds, and trauma don't just reside in the mind—they are stored in the nervous system, manifesting as tension, anxiety, and exhaustion.

Jewels incorporates somatic and nervous system regulation practices into her coaching to help clients process emotions rather than suppress them. Through body-based techniques, clients learn to:

- Rewire their nervous system for safety and calm.
- Release emotional overwhelm instead of intellectualizing it.
- Move from burnout to a state where they can hold more success, joy, and love.

This approach allows women to reclaim their power from within, leading to profound and lasting transformation.

From Restaurant Franchise Owner to Transformational Coach

Jewels' entrepreneurial journey began as the owner of a major restaurant franchise, an experience that taught her valuable lessons about success and self-worth.

For ten years, she operated under high levels of stress and burnout, believing that more achievement would eventually lead to fulfillment. However, she realized that success without self-love is an empty pursuit.

Her philosophy, *"Loving Myself to Success,"* now guides her coaching practice. It means:

- Embracing mistakes with compassion instead of criticism.
- Listening to the body instead of pushing through exhaustion.
- Celebrating small wins, not just major achievements.
- Incorporating rest and joy into the journey rather than delaying happiness for later.

Now, Jewels helps other women redefine success, ensuring it is built on a foundation of self-love and well-being rather than stress and sacrifice.

Self-Love in Leadership: Cultivating Success with Ease and Joy

Jewels Lamm's work is a powerful reminder that success is not something to be chased; it is something to be embodied. Through InBody: Rewire For Love and Connection, she empowers women to break free from perfectionism, control, and self-doubt, guiding them toward a life of fulfillment, joy, and radiant success. By restoring love within, women can step into their highest potential, creating a ripple effect of transformation in every area of their lives.

With Jewels as a guide, women worldwide are learning to embrace their full selves, lead with love, and thrive in both business and life.

3 COMMON MONEY MISTAKES WOMEN MAKE—

And How to Overcome Them

By Tolulope S. Olaniyan

Money isn't just about numbers—it's about freedom, choices, and impact. As a qualified financial adviser, transformation coach, and finance professional with a background in economics, I've worked with countless women who feel stuck in their financial journey. I see the same patterns over and over—brilliant, hardworking women struggling with money, not because they lack ambition, but because no one taught them how to take control of their finances and build lasting wealth.

As a Black Irish woman, I understand the unique challenges we face—balancing responsibilities, breaking generational cycles, and navigating financial systems that weren't always designed for us. That's why I'm passionate about helping women shift from financial survival to financial success. I don't just talk about money—I teach, coach, and empower women to thrive beyond borders—because financial freedom is for all of us.

If you've ever felt like money slips through your fingers no matter how hard you work, or you avoid financial conversations out of fear, you're not alone. But today, we're breaking that cycle. Let's talk about three common money mistakes women make and how to fix them—because you deserve financial peace and power.

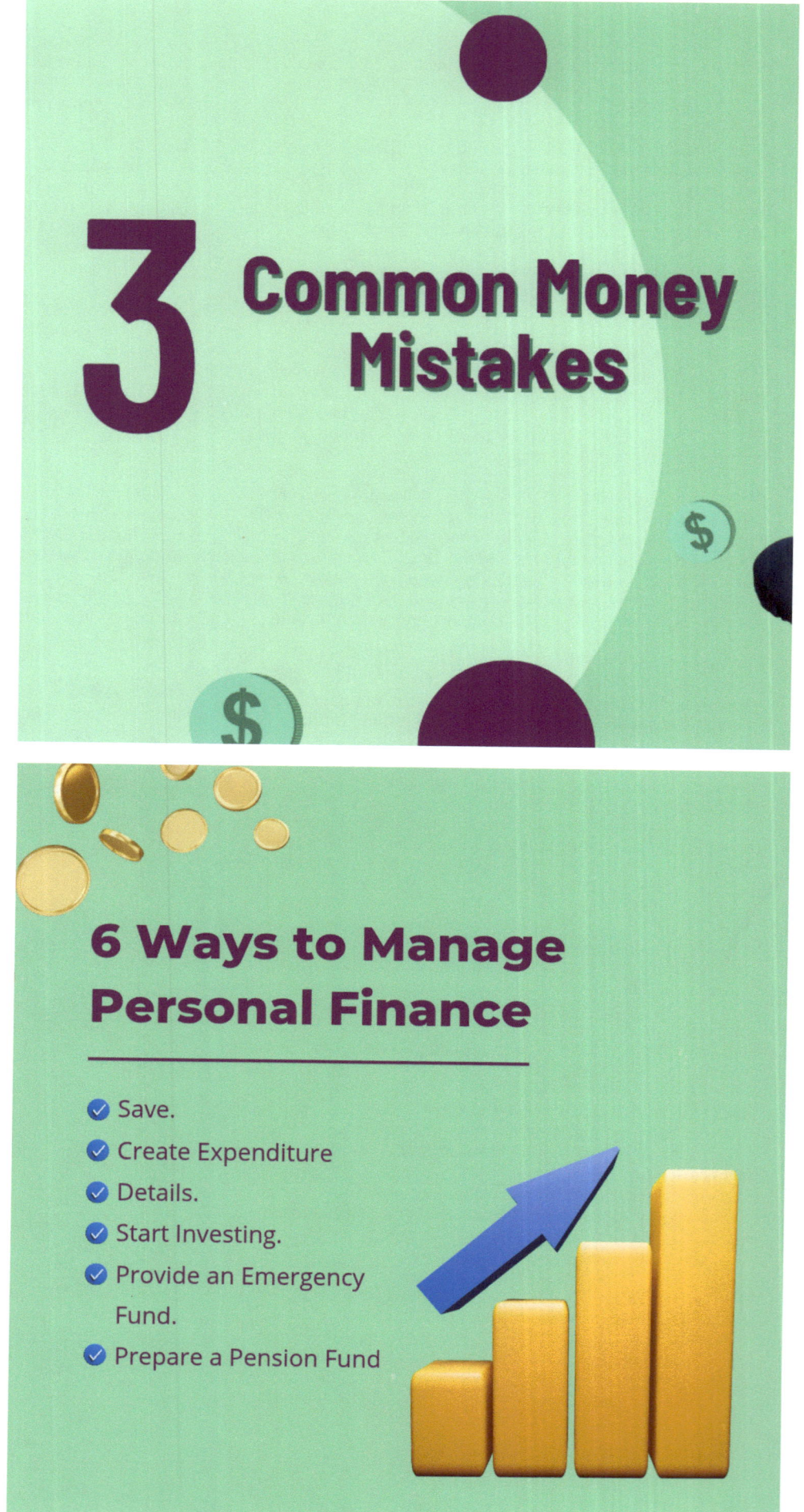

1. Avoiding Money Conversations

Women are amazing at handling responsibilities, but when it comes to discussing money—whether negotiating a salary, setting boundaries, or planning for the future—many of us hesitate. Why? Because we were conditioned to believe money talk is uncomfortable or *"not for us."*

The Cost of This Mistake: Avoiding financial conversations means missing out on opportunities—higher pay, better deals, and smarter financial decisions.

What you can do

- Normalize money talks. Discuss finances openly with your partner, friends, or a mentor. We break cycles by breaking the silence.
- Negotiate with confidence. Whether it's for a raise, business deal, or even household expenses, your financial well-being matters.
- Educate yourself. Take a financial course, join a money mastermind, or work with a coach (like me!) to boost your money confidence.

2. Not Having a Financial Plan

Many women focus on daily expenses but don't think long-term. The result? Living paycheck to paycheck, struggling with debt, or feeling financially stuck. A plan isn't just about saving—it's about building wealth and creating options.

The Cost of This Mistake: Without a plan, it's easy to overspend, under-save, and miss opportunities to grow your wealth.

What you can do:

- Create a budget that fits your life. Forget rigid spreadsheets—use a flexible, personalized system that works for YOU.
- Set clear financial goals. Whether it's buying a home, investing, or retiring early, clarity makes saving and earning easier.
- Build an emergency fund. Aim for 3-6 months of expenses as a safety net. Life happens—be prepared.

3. Relying on One Income Stream

One paycheck? One source of income? That's financial risk. Job loss, economic shifts, or unexpected expenses can shake your financial stability if you don't have a backup plan.

The Cost of This Mistake: No financial cushion means more stress, fewer choices, and a slower path to wealth.

- Diversify your income. Explore side hustles, freelancing, investments, or leveraging your skills for extra cash flow.
- Look into passive income. Rental properties, stocks, digital products, or affiliate marketing can make you money while you sleep.
- Invest in yourself. The best asset? YOU. Take courses, expand your skills, and open doors to higher-paying opportunities.

Take Back Your Financial Power

Women are powerful wealth-builders. The moment we start owning our financial journey, everything changes—more security, more freedom, more impact. And, when women thrive financially, we change the world.

Connect With Tolulope

www.eventaal.com
www.facebook.com/profile.php?id=100015001145314

THE POWER OF CONNECTION:

Building a Support System to Catapult Your Growth

By Sonia Rodrigues

It wasn't until I joined the She Rises Studios networking group and a few others that I truly understood the true power of surrounding myself with like-minded, driven women. I had spent so much time trying to do everything on my own—taking on every task, managing all the details—that I had forgotten that real growth happens in community. Trying to do everything on my own kept me from making progress in a way that I needed. The journey of entrepreneurship can feel incredibly isolating at times, but when you connect with others who are walking similar paths, you realize you are not alone. In fact, you also realize that you gain more momentum when you have the right supports in place and can bounce your ideas off of others. I found support and the motivation I needed to push things forward quickly when I connected with other women who could serve as a resource. Things I was stuck on shifted the minute I asked others for advice. These women offered wisdom, advice, and encouragement that catapulted my business forward in so many ways. What I learned is that mentorship doesn't always come from a single individual—it can come from an entire network of women who share their experiences and guidance, allowing you to learn from each other's successes and struggles.

Having a strong support system has been instrumental in my growth. When you invest in building meaningful relationships with mentors and peers, you unlock a wealth of knowledge and strength that accelerates your personal and professional development. You can achieve so much more when you find the right connections than you can alone.

Here are some tips I've learned along my journey that can help you take the first steps or move forward toward achieving your goals:

- **Believe in Your Potential:** One of the most powerful lessons I've learned is the importance of believing in yourself. Confidence in your abilities can carry you through even the toughest challenges. There will be obstacles for sure but if you stay connected to your vision and believe that you are capable, you will rise above any challenge you face. Keep pushing forward and ask lots of questions because chances are others have encountered the same obstacles and they can help you navigate through them.
- **Surround Yourself with the Right People:** Building a strong support network has been essential to my success. I can't emphasize enough how important it is to connect with women who share big dreams like you do. Seek out mentors, the right people can offer guidance, support, and inspiration, helping you learn faster and navigate the ups and downs of entrepreneurship with more confidence.
- **Create a Clear and Detailed Plan of Action:** One of the things that kept me moving forward was having a detailed vision and plan. Breaking down bigger goals into smaller, intentional steps kept me on track. Whether it was learning a new skill, investing in my business, or seeking guidance, I learned that consistent progress—no matter how small—leads to lasting success. Don't worry about being perfect, just keep moving forward, one very small step at a time and then celebrate those wins!
- **Build a Community of Women in Business:** Entrepreneurship doesn't have to be a lonely road. Surrounding yourself with like-minded, ambitious women who understand your struggles and share your goals, you create a space for collaboration, encouragement, and growth. Your community can help you stay motivated, inspired, and accountable. You can accomplish so much more when you are part of a network of other women who are all focused on scaling up.

The power of sisterhood cannot be overstated. As women, we are an unstoppable force when we unite, supporting and encouraging one another to reach our full potential.

We rise together, not by competing against each other, but by recognizing that there is enough space for all of us to thrive. Find strength in your community, learning from one another, and celebrating each other's successes. When we connect with one another, we are empowered to move past challenges and create the lives and businesses we have always dreamed of. So here's your reminder to keep dreaming, keep growing, and always remember—you are never alone in this journey, find your power in connection!

Connect With Sonia

www.linkedin.com/in/sonia-rodrigues-48b87149
www.facebook.com/SoniaRodriguesLPC
www.instagram.com/transition.to.wellness
www.transitiontowellness.com
www.latinxtherapy.com/therapists/sonia-rodrigues-marto-ma-lpc-lmft-lcadc-acs

FENIX TECH

MARK ZUCKERBERG:

Redefining Digital Connection in the App Age

Mark Zuckerberg has transformed the digital landscape, fundamentally altering the way people connect, communicate, and share information. As the co-founder of Facebook and the driving force behind its expansion into Instagram and WhatsApp, he has played a pivotal role in shaping the modern era of social networking. His vision has not only redefined social interactions but has also influenced app development on a global scale, setting new standards for user engagement, data-driven personalization, and platform integration.

From its humble beginnings in a Harvard dormitory to becoming a tech giant with billions of active users, Facebook's rise under Zuckerberg's leadership has been nothing short of revolutionary. The platform was initially designed as a closed network for college students but quickly grew into a global phenomenon, fostering a new kind of digital socialization. Through continuous innovation, Facebook introduced features that became industry benchmarks—news feeds, real-time messaging, and targeted advertising—all of which have had a profound impact on the app ecosystem.

Understanding the changing needs of users, Zuckerberg recognized the importance of visual storytelling in the digital age. This insight led to the acquisition of Instagram in 2012, a strategic move that capitalized on the growing trend of mobile photography and social sharing. Instagram's seamless interface and visually immersive experience redefined the way people consumed and engaged with content. By integrating AI-driven algorithms to curate personalized feeds, Zuckerberg helped set the foundation for modern app development, where customization and predictive analytics enhance user retention and engagement.

"The biggest risk is not taking any risk... In a world that is changing really quickly, the only strategy that is guaranteed to fail is not taking risks."

In 2014, Zuckerberg made another bold move by acquiring WhatsApp, a messaging app that had already gained traction due to its simplicity and end-to-end encryption. Recognizing the future of communication lay in mobile messaging rather than traditional social media, he ensured WhatsApp remained a standalone service while integrating elements of Facebook's monetization strategies. The platform became a vital tool for both personal and business communication, shaping the way enterprises interact with customers.

His contributions extend beyond individual applications. Under his leadership, Meta has pursued an interconnected ecosystem where apps function cohesively. The push towards the metaverse, an ambitious effort to redefine digital interaction through immersive virtual experiences, showcases his commitment to pushing the boundaries of app innovation. The development of augmented reality (AR) and virtual reality (VR) applications, including Meta's Horizon Worlds and the integration of VR with social networking, is a testament to his forward-thinking approach.

Zuckerberg's influence on app development also highlights the challenges of rapid digital expansion. Privacy concerns, data security issues, and regulatory scrutiny have emerged as critical discussions in the tech world, often centering around Facebook's handling of user information. These challenges have shaped industry-wide conversations about ethical app development, influencing policies and setting new standards for transparency and user consent.

Despite these challenges, Zuckerberg remains a dominant figure in shaping the future of digital communication. His ability to anticipate technological shifts and integrate emerging trends into mainstream applications has positioned him as one of the most influential figures in the app development landscape. Through Facebook, Instagram, and WhatsApp, he has not only changed how people connect but also established a blueprint for the next generation of transformative digital experiences.

SHE RISES
S T U D I O S

JOIN THE SRS COMMUNITY

WHERE WOMEN RISE TOGETHER!

Connect. Empower. Thrive. Whether you're an entrepreneur, professional, or simply seeking inspiration, **this is your space to grow!**

- Daily Motivation
- Expert Insights
- Sisterhood & Support

You don't have to do it alone—let's rise together!

JOIN NOW!

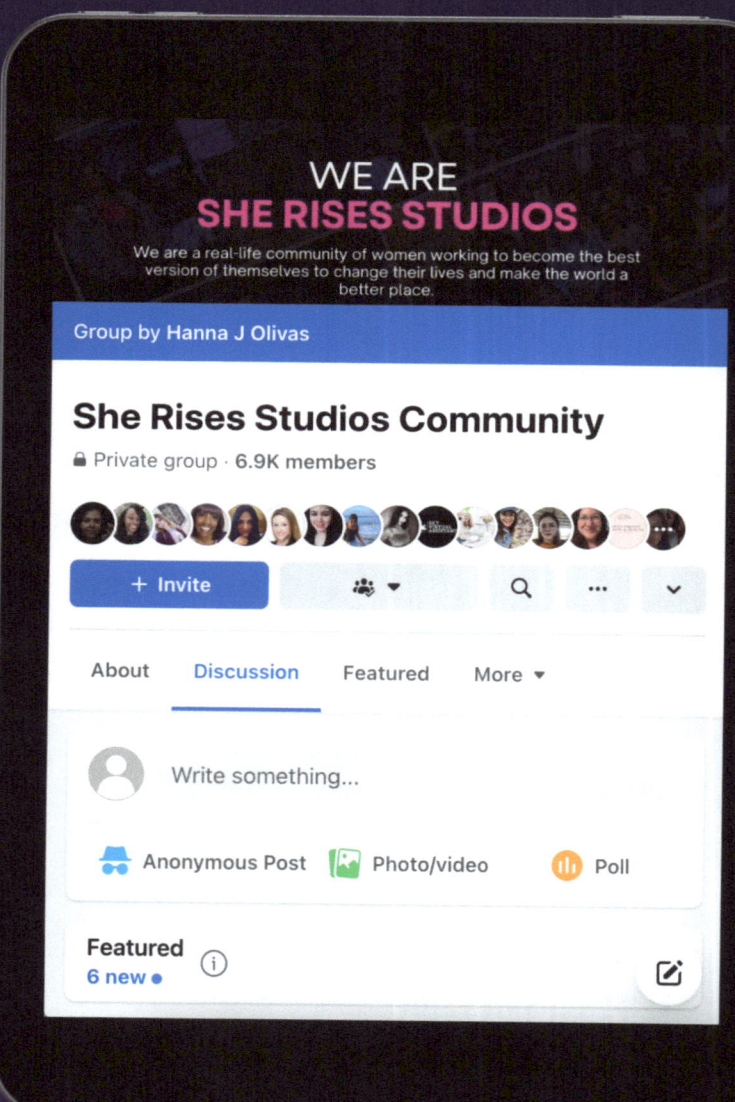

GRAB YOUR COPY NOW

WWW.AMAZON.COM/DP/1964619955

Pray, Don't Panic: The Path to Inner Calm offers a powerful collection of stories from women who have transformed fear into faith through prayer and trust. Led by Hanna Olivas and 25 inspiring authors, this book serves as a beacon of hope, showing how faith can guide us through life's toughest moments with grace and resilience.

Each chapter reminds us that choosing prayer over panic fosters inner peace, strength, and a deeper connection with our purpose. More than an anthology, this book is an invitation to embrace faith as the key to a calm and fulfilling life.

amazon.com   SHOP NOW   PUBLISHED BY
                                      SHE RISES
                                      STUDIOS

AI IN APP DEVELOPMENT:

A Powerful Tool for Human Connection

By Caitie Sfingi

Artificial intelligence has evolved from a buzzworthy concept to an essential tool in just a few years. For app developers, this shift presents an exciting opportunity to use AI not just as a technical feature but as a bridge for meaningful human connection. By leveraging AI, apps now have the potential to transform how we work, build relationships, and manage our lives with new ways that foster collaboration, understanding, and community.

At Merakite, we've been helping founders and companies turn their ideas into reality since 2017, and the rise of AI has opened up enormous possibilities for our clients. Here's how AI is creating innovative solutions while keeping the *"human"* at the heart of technology.

Where AI Meets Human-Centered App Design

Most people think of AI as being the opposite of human connection—cold, calculated, and impersonal (it is essentially just lots of math, after all). But as we've seen time and time again, the most successful AI-driven apps are the ones that amplify human experience rather than replace it.

One example of how AI algorithms can strengthen relationships is by supporting smarter matchmaking in networking apps or dating platforms. Imagine an app that doesn't just list potential contacts but connects users based on complementary goals, skill sets, or even shared career journeys. This kind of AI-powered feature doesn't just automate; it actually enriches interactions.

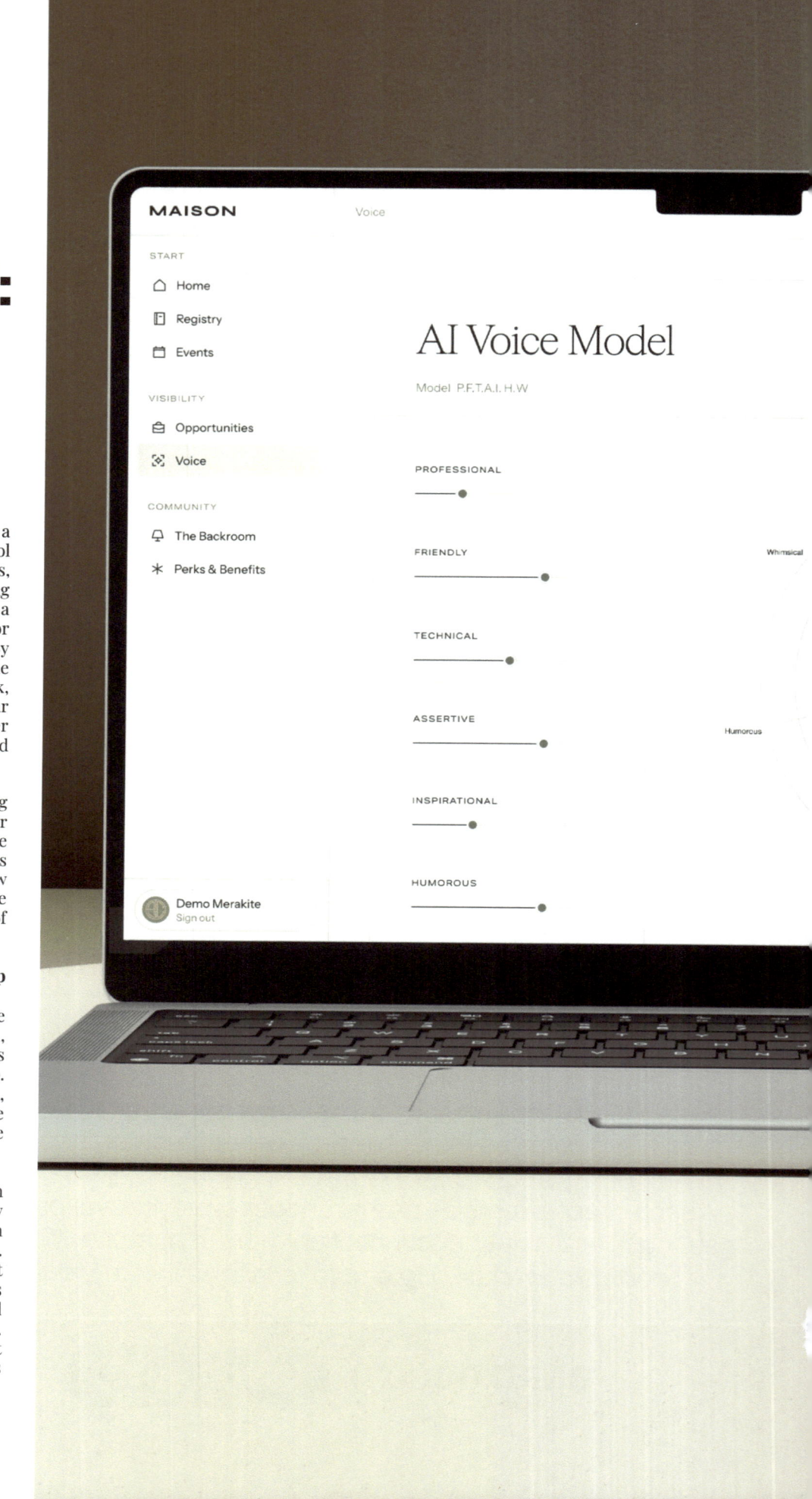

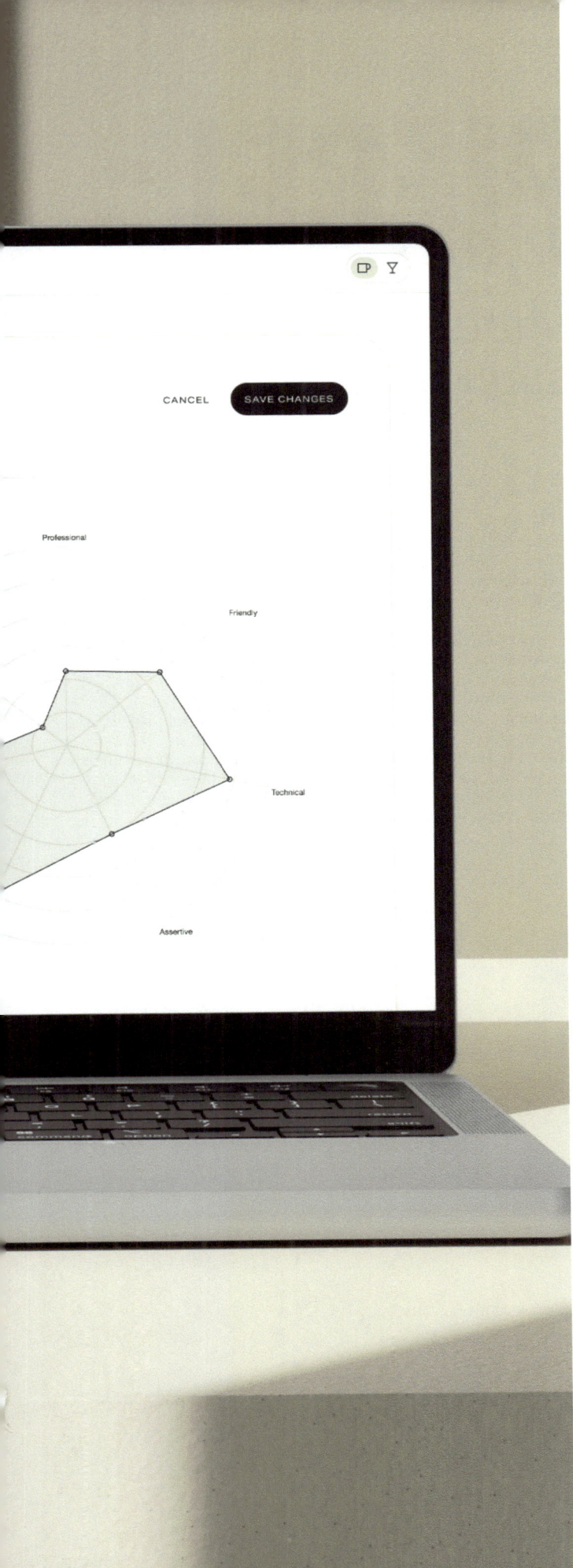

Similarly, AI can make digital conversations feel more intuitive. Chat apps today are a staple of communication, but anyone who's joined a bustling group chat knows how easy it is to fall behind. AI-powered summaries can help users stay in the loop, offering concise recaps that allow them to jump back into discussions with context, rather than scrolling endlessly to catch up.

But it's not just about improving our digital lives. AI is also making a big impact on how we work together in person. From smart scheduling tools that find the best meeting times for everyone involved, to virtual assistants that can handle mundane tasks like note-taking and transcription, AI is freeing up valuable time and energy for more meaningful human interactions.

This is what AI does best when paired with thoughtful app design—it removes barriers to connection, simplifies complexity, and encourages collaboration.

The Benefits of AI-Driven Development in Your App

Adding AI isn't just a shiny feature to pitch—it's a strategic move for app developers looking to make a long-term impact. Here's why AI is worth the investment for many products.

1. Incorporating Personalization at Scale

AI can analyze patterns and preferences to deliver personalized user experiences. Instead of a one-size-fits-all approach, apps with AI make users feel uniquely understood, whether it's delivering tailored recommendations or creating human-like interactions.

2. Streamlining Complex Tasks

From predictive analytics to automated workflows, AI reduces the friction of multitasking. For example, an AI budgeting app doesn't just categorize spending—it predicts cash flow issues, helping users make informed decisions that require less effort. Especially if you have a team that's prone to burnout or administrative burden, this can be a huge win for the people (yes, humans) who keep your business running.

3. Fostering Connection in a Digital World

Above all, the right application of AI helps build bridges between users. Whether improving communication across teams or facilitating meaningful personal introductions, AI tools reinforce connection in ways that feel more organic and human, not less. By incorporating AI into your app, you can create a more positive and engaging experience for users.

How to Leverage AI for More Human-Centric Apps

AI is revolutionizing app development, not by replacing human connection but by enhancing it. At Merakite, we're firm believers that the best technology empowers people—it simplifies lives, strengthens relationships, and bridges gaps.

As technology continues to advance, integrating AI into apps will become even more crucial for success. By keeping an open mind and staying updated on the latest developments, you can make your app stand out in a world where personalization and efficiency are key.

Connect With Caitie

www.merakite.com
www.instagram.com/merakite

EVAN SPIEGEL:

Pioneering the Future of Social Engagement Through Snapchat

Evan Spiegel has redefined digital communication, introducing a new paradigm for social interaction through Snapchat. As the co-founder of the ephemeral messaging platform, Spiegel has demonstrated a deep understanding of how users, particularly younger generations, engage with technology. His vision has not only set Snapchat apart in a competitive landscape dominated by Facebook and Instagram but has also influenced broader trends in app development, including augmented reality (AR), short-form content, and privacy-centric social networking.

When Snapchat was launched in 2011, it disrupted the traditional model of social media. Unlike platforms that prioritized permanent posts and meticulously curated profiles, Snapchat introduced the concept of disappearing messages, encouraging spontaneous and authentic interactions.

This fundamental shift in how people communicated digitally resonated deeply, particularly with younger users who sought a more private and less permanent way to engage online. Spiegel's approach was radical at the time, challenging the notion that all digital content should be archived indefinitely.

Under Spiegel's leadership, Snapchat evolved beyond messaging, transforming into a multimedia powerhouse that merged entertainment, advertising, and user engagement. The introduction of Stories in 2013 was a defining moment for the platform, allowing users to share photos and videos that disappeared after 24 hours. This innovation became so influential that it was later adopted by Instagram, Facebook, and even YouTube. The idea of temporary yet immersive content became a new standard in app development, shaping the way social media platforms structured user experiences.

"It's important to be thoughtful and mindful about the things you say to other people."

Another key contribution of Spiegel's vision is Snapchat's pioneering role in augmented reality. The platform's interactive lenses and filters revolutionized how users engaged with digital content, blurring the lines between reality and virtual enhancements. These AR innovations extended beyond entertainment, influencing sectors such as fashion, e-commerce, and even education. Brands quickly leveraged Snapchat's technology to create immersive advertising experiences, proving that AR could be seamlessly integrated into mobile applications for both personal and commercial use.

Snapchat also introduced Discover, a curated space for media companies, influencers, and brands to share high-quality content in a mobile-friendly format. This move signified a shift in how news and entertainment were consumed, embracing vertical video and interactive storytelling long before other platforms fully adopted these formats. Spiegel's ability to anticipate changing media consumption habits cemented Snapchat's position as a leader in mobile-first content innovation. Despite facing intense competition from industry giants like Meta, Spiegel has remained steadfast in preserving Snapchat's core identity. While other platforms have leaned towards algorithm-driven content and ad-heavy interfaces, Snapchat has maintained its focus on user privacy, direct communication, and creativity. This dedication to an authentic user experience has kept Snapchat relevant, particularly among Gen Z users who continue to value its unique approach to social interaction.

Beyond the success of Snapchat, Spiegel's work exemplifies how app development can shape digital culture. His commitment to innovation, coupled with an intuitive understanding of user behavior, has led to the creation of an app that not only entertains but also fosters genuine human connection. As technology continues to evolve, his contributions to the world of social media and app development will remain influential, pushing the boundaries of what is possible in digital communication.

THE RISE OF AI-DRIVEN APPS:

What's Next?

By Arias WebsterBerry

Artificial Intelligence isn't just shaping the future—it's defining it. AI-driven apps are evolving beyond simple automation and personalization. They're becoming intuitive, decision-making tools that enhance how we work, shop, and interact. From virtual assistants predicting our needs before we even speak to AI-powered medical diagnostics reshaping healthcare, the next wave of AI apps isn't just about convenience—it's about transformation.

AI-driven apps have already disrupted industries, but we're only scratching the surface. The real question isn't whether AI will dominate the app landscape—it's how it will evolve and what businesses must do to stay ahead.

The New Era of AI Apps: Beyond Automation

For years, AI in apps was mostly about automation/ chatbots, recommendation engines, and predictive analytics. But now, AI is moving beyond simple tasks into deeper cognitive capabilities.

- **Self-Learning Algorithms**: Apps are evolving to learn from the user instead of just reacting to them. AI-powered tools like ChatGPT, MidJourney, and Adobe Sensei aren't just responding to inputs—they're adapting to behaviors, preferences, and intent.
- **Real-Time AI Decision Making**: AI apps are now making complex, real-time decisions. In finance, AI-powered trading apps analyze market data instantly and execute trades faster than any human could. In customer service, AI agents are resolving issues with natural language understanding that rivals human conversation.
- **AI in No-Code & Low-Code Development**: AI is democratizing app development, making it possible for non-developers to build powerful applications with no-code platforms. AI-generated code suggestions and automated debugging are streamlining development cycles like never before.

The rise of AI-driven apps isn't just about making things faster—it's about making them smarter.

Industries AI-Driven Apps Are Disrupting Right Now

AI is rapidly shifting entire industries. Here's where we're seeing the most innovation:

- **Healthcare**: AI-powered medical apps are diagnosing diseases personalizing treatment plans and even assisting in surgeries. Apps like SkinVision use AI to detect skin cancer risks, while AI-driven diagnostic tools are outperforming human doctors in early disease detection.
- **E-Commerce & Retail**: Personalization has been taken to the next level. AI-powered shopping assistants analyze customer behavior in real-time to deliver tailored recommendations, predictive pricing, and even AI-driven styling advice.
- **Marketing & Content Creation**: AI isn't just optimizing ads—it's creating them. AI-powered apps like Jasper AI and Synthesia generate written and video content on demand, allowing businesses to scale content creation like never before.
- **Finance & Investing**: Robo-advisors like Wealthfront and Betterment are using AI to make investment decisions based on real-time market analysis democratizing wealth-building opportunities for everyday consumers.
- **Education & Learning**: AI tutors are now providing students with real-time feedback, adaptive learning paths, and personalized study plans. Platforms like Duolingo use AI to refine language learning, adapting difficulty levels based on individual progress.

If AI is already reshaping these industries, imagine where we'll be in just five years.

What's Next for AI-Driven Apps?

The future of AI-powered applications will be defined by three major shifts:

1. AI-Generated Apps
2. AI is no longer just inside apps—it's building them. AI-powered development platforms will soon allow businesses to describe an idea in natural language, and AI will generate the app framework, UI, and backend code in minutes.
3. Hyper-Personalization with Predictive AI
4. Apps will anticipate what users want before they even ask. AI will refine recommendations, automate decision-making, and create user experiences so seamless that they'll feel like second nature.
5. AI That Understands Emotion & Intent
6. The next evolution of AI will go beyond logic and into emotion. AI-driven apps will analyze tone, sentiment, and behavior, adjusting responses and experiences based on the user's emotions and state of mind. This could revolutionize customer service, mental health apps, and even AI-powered companionship tools.

By 2030, AI-powered apps won't just be tools they'll be partners in our daily lives.

The Challenge: AI Ethics, Bias, and Control

With great power comes great responsibility. As AI-driven apps become more advanced, so do the ethical dilemmas surrounding them.

- **Bias in AI Decision-Making**: AI models are only as unbiased as the data they're trained on. If companies don't implement rigorous checks, AI-powered decision-making can reinforce existing inequalities.
- **Privacy & Data Security**: AI apps thrive on data. The more they know about users, the better they perform—but at what cost? Striking a balance between personalization and privacy will be a defining challenge in AI app development.

- **AI Regulation & Control**: Governments and tech leaders are already pushing for AI regulations to prevent misuse. The companies that succeed will be those that build AI systems that are transparent, ethical, and user-first.

The AI arms race is well underway, but only the companies that prioritize trust and responsibility will win long-term.

Final Thoughts

AI-driven apps aren't a trend—they're the future of digital interaction. The businesses that embrace AI 1st development will lead the next wave of innovation, while those that resist will be playing catch-up.

We're heading into an era where AI isn't just supporting us—it's actively shaping our decisions, workflows, and even our creativity. The companies that master AI-driven app development today will define the future of every industry tomorrow.

The question isn't whether AI-driven apps will dominate the future. The question is—are you ready for it?

Connect With Arias

www.ariaswebsterberry.com
www.linkedin.com/in/ariaswebsterberry
www.instagram.com/ariaswebsterberry
www.twitter.com/AriasWBerry

Ultimate Comfort for Gaming & Scrolling

Plush Phone Holder With Secret Storage

- **Arthritis & Chronic Pain**
- **Kids & Teens**
- **Travelers**
- **The Disability Community**
- **Power Bank Users**
- **People Recovering from Illness**
- **Potato-Obsessed People**

Power Bank Sold Separately

PHONE SPUDS

Pillow · Phone Case · Power Bank

www.phonespuds.com

INSPIRE
EMPOWER
EDUCATE

JACK *DORSEY:*

Transforming Finance Through Mobile Innovation

Jack Dorsey has redefined the intersection of finance and technology, pioneering a new era of digital transactions through Square. As the co-founder and CEO of the fintech giant, Dorsey has leveraged his deep understanding of mobile app development to revolutionize the way businesses and individuals engage with financial services. His ability to blend sleek, user-friendly interfaces with powerful financial tools has not only democratized commerce but has also set new industry standards for accessibility, security, and innovation in mobile payments.

Square was founded in 2009 with a simple yet transformative vision: to empower small businesses by making digital payments seamless and accessible. At a time when traditional point-of-sale systems were cumbersome and costly, Dorsey introduced a compact card reader that could be plugged into a smartphone, instantly converting it into a mobile payment terminal. This innovation allowed independent sellers, artisans, and small business owners to process credit card transactions with ease, eliminating barriers that had previously hindered their ability to compete in a digital economy.

"Everything we do is about getting people to be more open, more creative, more courageous."

The success of Square was not solely rooted in hardware but in the sophisticated mobile applications that supported it. With an emphasis on intuitive design, the Square app provided businesses with real-time analytics, invoicing solutions, and inventory management tools—all accessible from a smartphone or tablet. This mobile-first approach to financial technology set Square apart from traditional banking institutions, positioning it as a leader in the evolving fintech landscape.

Dorsey's influence extended beyond small business solutions. Recognizing the shift towards peer-to-peer transactions, Square launched Cash App, a mobile payment service that redefined personal finance. By simplifying money transfers, enabling direct deposits, and even offering cryptocurrency trading, Cash App evolved into more than just a payment platform—it became a comprehensive financial ecosystem. Its rise in popularity demonstrated Dorsey's ability to anticipate digital trends and adapt financial services to the changing behaviors of consumers.

His vision for financial inclusion also played a significant role in shaping Square's long-term strategy. Unlike traditional banking systems that often cater to established businesses and high-income users, Square and Cash App provided financial tools to underserved communities, freelancers, and independent workers. Features like instant payouts and fractional stock investing allowed users to take control of their financial futures, reinforcing Dorsey's commitment to bridging the gap between technology and accessibility.

Beyond innovation, Square's impact on the broader app development space is undeniable. The seamless integration of machine learning for fraud detection, blockchain technology for cryptocurrency transactions, and AI-driven financial insights set a new benchmark for fintech applications. Dorsey's approach proved that financial apps could be both sophisticated and user-friendly, reshaping consumer expectations and influencing the next generation of mobile financial services.

Despite stepping away from his role at Twitter, Dorsey remains a formidable force in the tech industry, continuing to push the boundaries of what mobile apps can achieve in the financial sector. His work with Square has not only modernized commerce but has also demonstrated the transformative power of mobile-first financial solutions. As digital transactions continue to evolve, Dorsey's contributions will serve as a foundation for the future of fintech, ensuring that financial technology remains accessible, innovative, and deeply integrated into the digital economy.

ZOOMBINIS:

A *Visionary Blend* of *Creativity* and *Technology* in *Educational Gaming*

Long before *"computational thinking"* became a cornerstone of STEM education, a group of little blue creatures were training young minds in logic, pattern recognition, and problem-solving. Inspired by 1990s research on data literacy and visual exploration tools, Broderbund and TERC developed Logical Journey of the Zoombinis—a game that wasn't just fun but also established the foundations of algorithmic reasoning.

Released in 1996, Zoombinis was a breakout hit in the edutainment space, selling over half a million copies and spawning sequels. But its true legacy goes beyond sales numbers. Many fans recognize the game for igniting their passion for coding, AI, and data science, while educators—some even keeping outdated computers running just to preserve access—recognized its unique ability to teach logic through play.

Fast forward to the 21st century: as demand for computational thinking boomed, the Zoombinis were revived. TERC partnered with FableVision Studios and Learning Games Network to reimagine the game for modern platforms in 2015. Now, in collaboration with FableVision Games, Zoombinis is making its way into classrooms, backed by research proving its effectiveness as a teaching tool.

At a time when game-play is reshaping learning, Zoombinis remains a powerful example of how play and problem-solving can intersect—years ahead of its time and still shaping the future.

About the Partners Behind the Revival

TERC is a nonprofit made up of teams of math and science education, and research experts dedicated to innovation and creative problem-solving. At the forefront of theory and practice, TERC's work encompasses research, content and curriculum development, technology innovation, professional development, and program evaluation. Passionate about social justice, TERC strives to create level playing fields for all learners, reaching more than three million students every year. To learn more, visit *www.terc.edu.*

FableVision Studios creates award-winning games, animated films, museum kiosks, apps, websites, and more—helping to shape a more innovative and compassionate world.

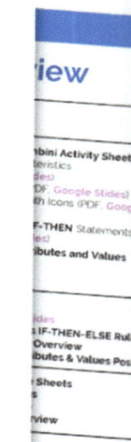

Their signature blend of positive messaging, storytelling, and interactive technologies is sought after by leading publishers, broadcasters, educational organizations, nonprofits, museums, and healthcare organizations. To learn more, visit *www.fablevisionstudios.com.*

By identifying and partnering with organizations that create, research, and distribute game-based learning tools, the Learning Games Network amplifies the impact of educational games and broadens access for learners of all ages. To learn more, visit *www.learninggamesnetwork.org.*

Zoombinis in the Classroom

Zoombinis, an educational game featuring twelve math-based logic puzzles with four levels of difficulty, serving as an engaging tool for developing essential computational thinking skills. By guiding the adorable blue beings through a series of challenges, students practice problem decomposition—breaking down complex tasks into manageable parts—as well as automation, where they predict and sequence order steps for efficient solutions. The game reinforces algorithmic thinking by encouraging players to search out and apply structured sets of instructions, while also honing their ability to interpret and utilize various forms of data representation. Additionally, Zoombinis fosters abstraction and formulation, helping students recognize patterns and develop generalizable problem-solving strategies. By encouraging learners to apply common algorithms across diverse scenarios, the game nurtures a strong foundation in logical reasoning, making it an innovative and effective resource for the modern classroom.

Zoombinis Clubs: Engaging After-School Learning Through Play

Zoombinis Clubs offer an exciting opportunity for after-school programs, informal learning spaces, and out-of-school-time initiatives to bring computational thinking to life. Designed to complement the beloved, research-based Zoombinis game, these clubs provide hands-on, offline activities that promote collaboration and problem-solving in a fun, engaging way.

With 10 hours of structured in-person programming alongside online gameplay, Zoombinis Clubs empower students in grades 3-7 to strengthen their math and logic skills while enjoying the game's timeless appeal.

The interactive activities include:
- **Make Your Own Zoombini** – Creative character design
- **Allergic Cliffs: Act It Out** – Understanding logical relationships
- **Pizza Pass: Organizing Data** – Sorting and categorization
- **Fleens: What's My Rule?** – Identifying patterns and rules
- **Captain Cajun's Ferryboat: Act It Out** – Sequencing and decision-making

Each club kit comes with a facilitator's guide, printable PDF resources, Google Slides presentations, and adaptable modifications for both small and large groups. Whether enhancing an existing program or launching a new learning initiative, Zoombinis Clubs provide a dynamic way to inspire curiosity, critical thinking, and collaboration in young learners.

For those interested in the educational impact of Zoombinis, several online platforms provide valuable insights, resources, and community engagement. The official TikTok Zoombinis page (*@zoombinisgame*) features gameplay tips, behind-the-scenes content, and creative ways to incorporate the game into learning. On Facebook (*@ZoombinisGame*) and Instagram (*@zoombinis_game*), educators, parents, and fans can stay connected, share experiences, and discover new ways to use Zoombinis for building computational thinking skills. The TERC Zoombinis website (*terc.edu/zoombinis/*)offers in-depth research, educator resources, and guidance for integrating the game into classrooms and after-school programs. Whether you're a longtime fan or new to the world of Zoombinis, these platforms offer fresh ideas, expert insights, and a vibrant community dedicated to learning through play.

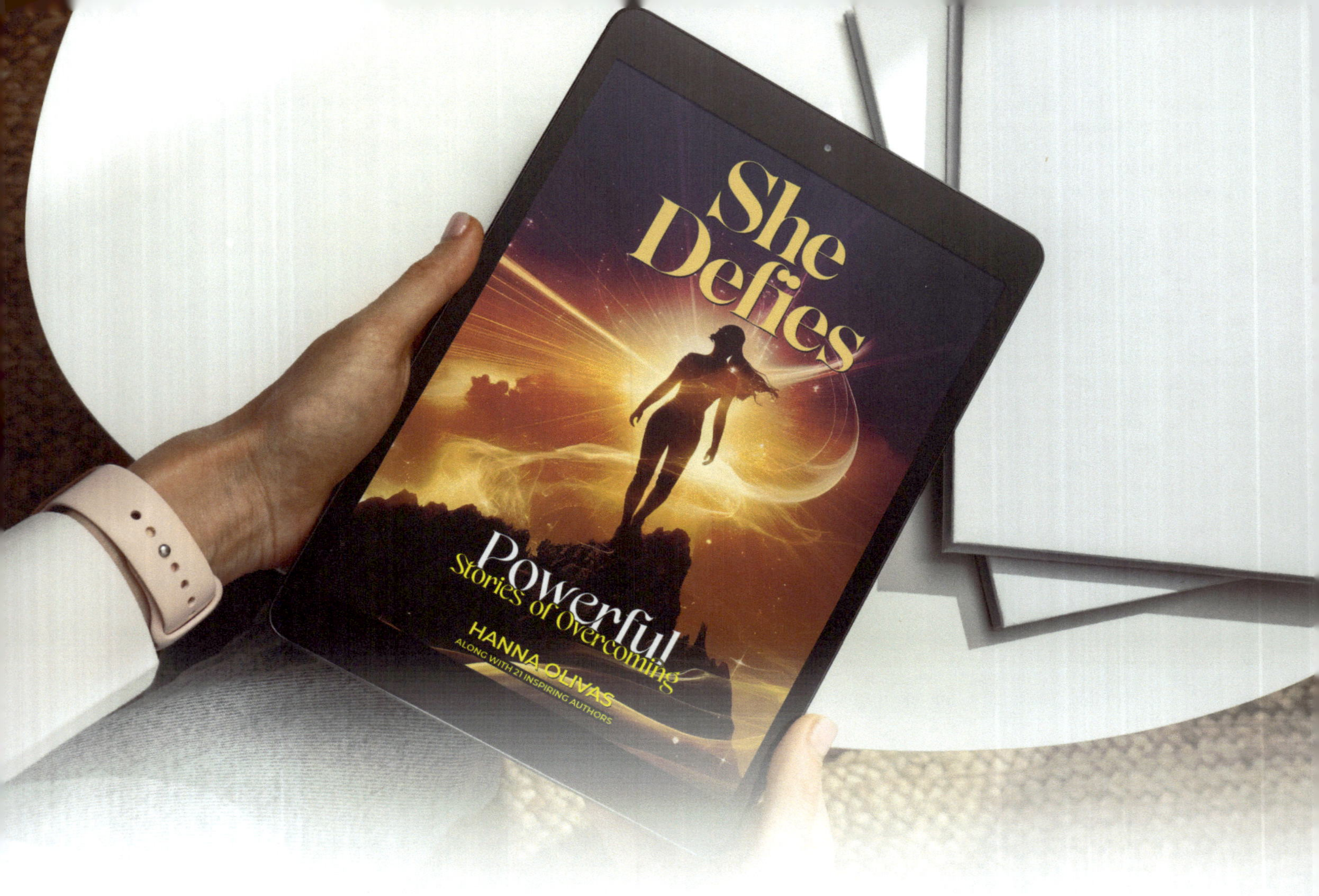

GRAB YOUR COPY NOW

WWW.AMAZON.COM/DP/1966798040

She Defies: Powerful Stories of Overcoming shares the raw, real journeys of 30 extraordinary women who have faced life's toughest challenges and emerged victorious. Led by Hanna Olivas and 21 inspiring authors, this book is a testament to the resilience, courage, and determination found within every woman. Through stories of perseverance —from overcoming personal loss to defying societal expectations—each chapter offers inspiration and strength.

A must-read for anyone seeking empowerment, She Defies reminds us that no matter what life throws our way, we all have the power to rise, overcome, and shine.

SHOP NOW

PUBLISHED BY

SHE RISES
S T U D I O S

GRAB YOUR COPY NOW

WWW.AMAZON.COM/DP/1964619939

Pray, Live, Lead by Faith: Faith-Fueled Success explores how faith serves as the foundation for success in life, business, family, health, and wealth. Hanna Olivas and co-authors Carmen K. Maendel, Shirley Marie, Erica Elliott, Yalonda Smith, and Ginny Jones share powerful stories of resilience, leadership, and transformation through faith.

This inspiring book, accompanied by a global docuseries, reveals how faith fuels balance, bold decision-making, and lasting success. A must-read for those seeking purpose, strength, and fulfillment in every aspect of life.

amazon.com   SHOP NOW   PUBLISHED BY
SHE RISES STUDIOS

SUNDAR PICHAI:

Driving Google's Innovation from Android to the Future of Apps

Sundar Pichai has been instrumental in shaping the modern app ecosystem, leading Google's transformation into a global powerhouse of mobile innovation. As the CEO of Google and its parent company Alphabet, Pichai has overseen the expansion of Android, the evolution of the Google Play Store, and the development of groundbreaking apps and services that define how billions of users interact with technology. His vision has not only solidified Google's dominance in the mobile space but has also pushed the boundaries of what app development can achieve in the digital age.

When Pichai joined Google in 2004, the company was primarily known for its search engine. However, he quickly rose through the ranks, leading key projects that would later become indispensable to Google's app ecosystem. His work on Google Chrome demonstrated his ability to anticipate user needs, creating a browser that seamlessly integrated speed, security, and functionality. This focus on user experience became a guiding principle as he took on larger roles within the company.

Pichai's influence on mobile app development became most apparent when he took charge of Android in 2013. Under his leadership, Android evolved from being just an operating system into a comprehensive digital ecosystem that powers the vast majority of the world's smartphones. By making Android open-source and accessible to a wide range of manufacturers, he ensured that mobile technology could reach even the most remote parts of the world. This democratization of smartphone access played a crucial role in expanding app development opportunities, enabling millions of developers to create applications that could reach global audiences.

One of Pichai's key contributions to app innovation is the refinement of the Google Play Store.

"For me, it matters that we drive technology as an equalizing force, as an enabler for everyone around the world. Which is why I do want Google to see, push, and invest more in making sure computing is more accessible, connectivity is more accessible."

Recognizing the need for a seamless, secure, and user-friendly app marketplace, he spearheaded initiatives to improve app discoverability, strengthen security measures, and enhance developer support. His emphasis on machine learning and AI-powered recommendations has made the Play Store not just a distribution platform but an intelligent marketplace that curates content based on user preferences. This approach has significantly increased engagement and retention, benefiting both users and developers.

Beyond Android and the Play Store, Pichai has driven innovation across Google's suite of apps, ensuring they remain at the forefront of technological advancements. From the evolution of Google Maps into a fully immersive navigation tool to the integration of AI-powered features in Google Photos, Docs, and Assistant, his leadership has emphasized the importance of smart, intuitive app experiences. By prioritizing AI and cloud computing, he has positioned Google's apps as essential tools in both personal and professional environments.

Pichai's impact extends beyond consumer applications. His push for progressive web apps and cloud-based solutions has redefined how businesses operate in a mobile-first world. With initiatives like Google Workspace and Firebase, he has provided developers and enterprises with the tools needed to build scalable, efficient applications that cater to modern digital demands. His vision for a seamlessly interconnected ecosystem has made it easier for businesses to integrate mobile technology into their operations.

At a time when privacy and security concerns are at the forefront of technological discussions, Pichai has championed efforts to make Google's app ecosystem safer and more transparent. Initiatives like the Google Play Protect system and stronger data protection policies reflect his commitment to maintaining user trust while fostering innovation.

Sundar Pichai's leadership has ensured that Google remains at the cutting edge of app development in an era defined by rapid digital transformation. His ability to anticipate industry shifts, embrace emerging technologies, and prioritize user-centric design has solidified Google's role as an innovation leader. As mobile technology continues to evolve, Pichai's influence will undoubtedly shape the future of app experiences, ensuring that Google remains a driving force in the digital revolution.

www.sherisesstudios.com

BRIAN CHESKY:

Redefining Travel Through Airbnb's Digital Revolution

Brian Chesky has transformed the global travel industry through Airbnb, an app that reimagined how people find accommodations and experience new destinations. As the co-founder and CEO, Chesky has leveraged mobile technology to create a seamless, community-driven platform that connects travelers with unique lodging options across the world. What began as a simple idea to rent out spare space has evolved into a multi-billion-dollar business that reshapes the way people travel, blending convenience, affordability, and personalized experiences through a digital-first approach.

The inception of Airbnb in 2008 was driven by a challenge Chesky and his co-founders faced—finding an affordable place to stay during a busy conference in San Francisco. Realizing that others might have similar needs, they developed a platform that allowed homeowners to list their spaces for short-term rental. However, it was through mobile app development that Airbnb truly revolutionized the hospitality industry. By enabling users to browse listings, communicate with hosts, and book stays directly from their smartphones, Chesky eliminated traditional barriers to travel planning and created a new model for lodging.

The Airbnb app is a testament to Chesky's commitment to user experience and innovation. Its intuitive interface allows travelers to explore accommodations through high-quality images, reviews, and personalized recommendations powered by AI. By integrating real-time messaging and secure payment processing, the app fosters trust between hosts and guests, ensuring a smooth and reliable transaction process. The ability to instantly book stays, manage itineraries, and receive local recommendations has made Airbnb more than just a booking platform—it has become an essential travel companion.

Beyond convenience, Airbnb has disrupted the hospitality industry by shifting the focus from standard hotel stays to unique, local experiences. Chesky's vision extended beyond lodging to the creation of Airbnb Experiences, an app-integrated feature that allows travelers to book curated activities hosted by locals. Whether it's a cooking class in Italy or a guided street art tour in Tokyo, this addition has positioned Airbnb as a platform that not only provides places to stay but also facilitates immersive cultural experiences.

Chesky's leadership has also propelled Airbnb into new frontiers, including extended stays and remote work accommodations. With the rise of digital nomadism, Airbnb adapted its platform to cater to long-term travelers, offering flexible booking options and remote work-friendly properties. This shift has enabled users to live and work from anywhere, reinforcing the app's role in the evolving travel landscape.

"Never assume you can't do something. Push yourself to redefine the boundaries."

Despite facing regulatory challenges and industry pushback, Chesky has maintained Airbnb's commitment to community-driven hospitality. The company's trust and safety measures, including identity verification, user reviews, and enhanced security features, have helped maintain credibility and ensure a positive experience for both hosts and guests. His emphasis on responsible tourism and sustainability has further positioned Airbnb as a forward-thinking leader in the travel sector.

Brian Chesky's impact on the travel and hospitality industry is undeniable. Through Airbnb, he has demonstrated how mobile technology can disrupt traditional business models, empower individuals, and redefine consumer expectations. As the world of travel continues to evolve, Chesky's innovative approach ensures that Airbnb remains at the forefront of digital hospitality, shaping the future of how people explore the world.

ALEXIS OHANIAN:

Shaping the Future of Community-Driven Content Through Mobile Innovation

Alexis Ohanian has played a pivotal role in transforming how people engage with digital communities through Reddit, a platform that has redefined online discussions, content sharing, and social interactions. As the co-founder of Reddit, Ohanian envisioned a space where users could freely exchange ideas, collaborate on interests, and participate in a constantly evolving ecosystem of conversations. While Reddit began as a simple website, its expansion into mobile technology has been instrumental in reshaping how people consume and interact with community-driven content in the digital age.

In an era where social media platforms prioritize algorithm-driven feeds, Reddit stands out as a user-led network allowing individuals to curate and control their experiences. Ohanian's early understanding of the power of online communities positioned Reddit as one of the internet's most influential hubs for discourse, knowledge-sharing, and viral trends. However, it was the shift toward mobile accessibility that truly propelled the platform into mainstream culture. Recognizing the need for a seamless, on-the-go experience, Reddit's transition into mobile app development ensured its continued relevance in an increasingly mobile-first world.

The Reddit app revolutionized how users engage with content, making discussions more interactive, immersive, and instantaneous. Unlike traditional social networks, where passive scrolling dominates, Reddit encourages deep participation through upvotes, comments, and subreddit communities. The app's intuitive design allows users to seamlessly navigate thousands of niche communities, receive real-time updates, and contribute to discussions with multimedia integration, including images, GIFs, and live streaming. By prioritizing a mobile-friendly interface, Ohanian and his team ensured that Reddit remained a space for organic conversations, whether users were browsing from desktops or smartphones.

One of the key innovations under Ohanian's leadership was enhancing mobile functionality to support real-time engagement. Features like push notifications, live threads, and interactive AMAs (Ask Me Anything) sessions have elevated user experiences, fostering a sense of immediacy and direct connection with content creators, industry experts, and global figures. This shift has made Reddit a powerful tool for breaking news, citizen journalism, and real-time event discussions, further solidifying its status as a go-to platform for raw, unfiltered information.

Beyond fostering conversations, Ohanian championed the development of Reddit's mobile monetization strategies, balancing user experience with revenue generation. While the platform initially thrived on organic, ad-free discussions, its mobile app introduced a refined advertising model that integrated promoted posts, native ads, and premium subscriptions like Reddit Premium. By ensuring that monetization efforts did not compromise the platform's authenticity, he helped Reddit maintain its grassroots appeal while expanding its business potential.

Reddit's influence extends beyond entertainment and social interactions—it has become a digital ecosystem that drives cultural movements, financial markets, and societal discourse. From the rise of meme stocks in r/WallStreetBets to global activism campaigns, Reddit's mobile accessibility has enabled users to mobilize in ways never seen before. Ohanian's foresight in embracing mobile technology ensured that Reddit was not just a platform for discussion but a catalyst for real-world impact.

Alexis Ohanian's contributions to the evolution of community-driven content highlight the transformative power of mobile technology. By prioritizing user engagement, accessibility, and real-time interaction, he helped Reddit transition from a niche forum to a digital powerhouse. As mobile technology continues to advance, Ohanian's vision of an open, participatory internet remains a driving force in shaping the future of online communities, proving that innovation thrives where people are empowered to connect, share, and create.

GRAB YOUR COPY NOW

HTTPS://WWW.AMAZON.COM/DP/1964619904

In Women Decision Makers: Women's Stories and Strategies in Decision-Making, Hanna Olivas, Adriana Luna Carlos, and co-authors Jacqueline Long, Tania Vasallo, Nermin Fathy, Megan Waite, and Megan Henry showcase how women are breaking barriers and shaping a more inclusive future. Through powerful stories and strategies, this book highlights the impact of diverse leadership across industries.

A must-read for those passionate about leadership, gender equality, and social change, it inspires action and celebrates the power of women in decision-making.

SHOP NOW

PUBLISHED BY
SHE RISES
STUDIOS

GRAB YOUR COPY NOW

WWW.AMAZON.COM/DP/1964619963

The Ultimate Wedding Guide: Expert Tips and Secrets for Your Dream Wedding takes the stress out of wedding planning with expert advice from top industry professionals. Hanna Olivas and co-authors Denise O'Malley, Kenya E. Aissa MS, Ashley McCombs, Candice Damele, Kristin Sullivan, Heather Arra, Callie Rackley Carr, Jean Neuhart, and Beverly Little share invaluable insights on budgeting, timelines, vendor selection, and personalized details to make your day unforgettable.

With real-life anecdotes, creative ideas, and step-by-step guidance, this essential resource helps you plan a seamless, joyful celebration.

SARAH LEARY:

Transforming Neighborhood Connections Through Nextdoor's Digital Innovation

Sarah Leary has redefined how communities connect through Nextdoor, the pioneering social network designed to bring neighbors closer together in a digital age. As the co-founder of the platform, Leary saw the potential for mobile technology to bridge the gap between physical neighborhoods and online communication, fostering a sense of belonging and trust among residents. Under her leadership, Nextdoor has evolved from a simple neighborhood forum into a global platform that facilitates local discussions, resource sharing, and community-driven solutions, fundamentally reshaping modern community engagement.

In an era where social media primarily focuses on global connectivity, Leary recognized an unmet need—local communities were becoming increasingly disconnected despite the rise of digital communication. Inspired by the idea that technology could help revive neighborhood engagement, she and her co-founders launched Nextdoor in 2011 as a private, hyperlocal platform where residents could share information, ask for recommendations, and support one another. The platform's success was largely fueled by its mobile-first approach, ensuring that users could access and contribute to their local communities anytime, anywhere.

Nextdoor's mobile app became the cornerstone of its success, offering a seamless, user-friendly interface that prioritized real-time, location-based interactions. Unlike traditional social networks that rely on expansive friend lists, Nextdoor connects users based on geographical proximity, ensuring that conversations remain relevant and meaningful to their everyday lives. This approach has made it an indispensable tool for local updates, from lost pets and community events to emergency alerts and neighborhood safety concerns.

One of Leary's key contributions to the platform was ensuring that it remained a trusted, secure space for residents. By implementing a rigorous verification system that requires users to prove residency in their designated neighborhood, she maintained the integrity of discussions and fostered a sense of accountability among members. This emphasis on authenticity set Nextdoor apart from other social platforms, reinforcing its role as a community-driven network rather than a traditional social media site.

Beyond facilitating conversations, Nextdoor has played a crucial role in crisis response and local government communication. Leary spearheaded partnerships with municipalities, law enforcement agencies, and emergency services, integrating features that allow officials to provide real-time updates directly to communities. Whether it's disaster preparedness, crime prevention, or civic engagement, the app has become a vital resource for public safety and local governance.

The platform's expansion into business engagement further solidified its place in the digital landscape. Recognizing that small businesses are the backbone of local economies, Leary helped introduce features that allow businesses to connect with nearby customers, promote services, and gather community-driven recommendations. By seamlessly integrating commerce with community engagement, Nextdoor has become a powerful tool for both residents and local entrepreneurs.

Sarah Leary's vision for Nextdoor goes beyond digital networking —it embodies the idea that technology can strengthen real-world relationships. By leveraging mobile innovation, she created a platform that not only connects neighbors but also empowers them to take an active role in shaping their communities. As mobile technology continues to evolve, Nextdoor's impact under Leary's leadership serves as a testament to how digital solutions can drive meaningful, localized change, ensuring that communities remain connected in an increasingly digital world.

FROM BURNOUT TO BREAKTHROUGH:

How I Reclaimed My Health, Purpose, and Power

By Monica Connolly

For much of my life, I was the one everyone relied on—the caregiver, provider, problem solver. I carried the weight of my family's needs, always showing up for others while ignoring my own body and spirit. I thought resilience meant pushing through, that strength was found in sacrifice. But that belief came at a cost.

My health crumbled under the pressure. Chronic pain and exhaustion became my normal. I numbed the emotional toll with food, overwork, and a relentless need to stay busy. I had lost myself in survival mode and no longer recognized the person in the mirror.

Then, I heard the words that changed everything: *"If you don't make drastic changes, you will die."*

That moment forced me to confront the truth—I wasn't just battling illness. I was carrying years of unprocessed trauma, emotional exhaustion, and an identity built around everyone else's needs but my own. I had two choices: keep going down the same path or rise and reclaim my life.

Healing wasn't just about losing weight or fixing symptoms. It was about rebuilding my entire foundation—mind, body, and spirit. I immersed myself in holistic health, uncovering the deep connection between gut health, emotional well-being, and the stress trapped in my body. As I transformed, I realized this wasn't just my battle—it was the story of countless women who had sacrificed themselves for others.

That realization sparked my mission. I became a certified holistic health and wellness coach, master life coach, and high-performance mentor—dedicated to helping others break free from burnout, self-doubt, and silent struggles. My journey wasn't just about reclaiming my own health—it was about creating a pathway for others to do the same. I knew that if I could rebuild my life, I could help others do it too.

Today, my work spans multiple avenues, all rooted in the same mission: helping people reclaim their health, confidence, and purpose.

As a transformation expert and mindset coach, I guide individuals through holistic healing, mindset shifts, and high-performance strategies to help them step into their full potential. Whether they're rebuilding after burnout, starting a business, or redefining their purpose, I equip them with the tools they need to thrive.

I also understand the power of community, which is why I created Ember to Empire, a women's networking collective designed for entrepreneurs building legacy businesses while prioritizing health and well-being. Connection is at the heart of transformation, and inside this space, women find support, collaboration, and inspiration to rise together.

Through The Unshakeable Belief Podcast, I share stories of resilience, healing, and reinvention. Each episode reminds us that no matter how hard life gets, we have the power to rise from the ashes and create a life aligned with our purpose. I believe that when we share our journeys, we empower others to take bold action in their own lives.

I never expected to be a speaker and mentor for others, but when you find your purpose, it becomes impossible to stay silent. Now, I share my story on stages across the country, inspiring others to take control of their health, mindset, and future. This year, I'm honored to speak at The Unstoppable Success Summit with Amberly Lago, The Impact Maker Summit, and many other transformational events—proving our struggles can fuel our greatest impact.

Looking back, I don't regret my past—I see it as the foundation of my mission. Everything I went through led me here, where I help others step into their own healing and power.

Because the truth is, resilience isn't just about surviving—it's about reclaiming your life, rewriting your story, and choosing to thrive.

Connect With Monica

www.monicaconnollycoaching.com
www.facebook.com/monica.a.connolly.7
www.linkedin.com/in/mnconnolly
www.instagram.com/monicaconnollyandco

TRAVIS *KALANICK*:

Driving the Future of Urban Mobility
Through Uber's App Revolution

"Fear is the disease. Hustle is the antidote Whatever it is that you're afraid of, go after it."

Travis Kalanick transformed the transportation industry with Uber, an app that reshaped urban mobility, disrupted traditional taxi services, and redefined how people move through cities. As the co-founder and former CEO, Kalanick played a critical role in leveraging mobile technology to create a seamless ride-hailing experience, forever altering the landscape of personal transportation. His vision for Uber was not just about convenience but about harnessing technology to make mobility more accessible, efficient, and scalable on a global scale.

Before Uber's launch in 2009, urban transportation was dominated by taxis and public transit, both of which had inefficiencies in availability, pricing, and accessibility. Kalanick recognized these gaps and saw an opportunity to streamline the process through a mobile-first solution. By integrating GPS tracking, real-time ride requests, and cashless transactions into a single platform, Uber eliminated the friction of traditional taxi services, allowing users to hail rides with the tap of a button. The simplicity and reliability of Uber's mobile app quickly gained traction, propelling it from a Silicon Valley startup to a global phenomenon.

One of Uber's most groundbreaking features was its dynamic pricing model, which adjusted fares based on demand, optimizing the availability of drivers while maximizing efficiency. While controversial, this approach showcased how mobile technology could revolutionize service-based industries by using real-time data analytics to balance supply and demand. Kalanick's aggressive expansion strategy ensured that Uber scaled rapidly, entering new markets and adapting to different regulatory landscapes, solidifying its position as a dominant force in ride-sharing.

Under Kalanick's leadership, Uber's app evolved beyond simple ride-hailing to incorporate new mobility solutions, such as UberPOOL for shared rides, UberEATS for food delivery, and Uber for Business, catering to corporate travel needs. Each innovation reinforced Uber's role as a technology-driven platform rather than just a transportation service. By continuously refining the app's interface, integrating AI-driven route optimization, and expanding payment options, Kalanick ensured that Uber remained at the forefront of the digital mobility revolution.

Beyond its convenience, Uber's impact on urban mobility has been profound. The app helped reduce reliance on car ownership, offering an alternative to expensive parking, maintenance, and insurance costs. It also provided new economic opportunities through its gig-based driver model, allowing individuals to earn income on flexible schedules. However, this disruption was not without controversy, as Uber faced scrutiny over labor practices, regulatory battles, and competitive tactics. Despite these challenges, Kalanick's ability to drive innovation and market expansion kept Uber ahead in an increasingly competitive landscape.

GET YOUR COPY NOW

Celebrate the power of women through inspiring stories and insights.

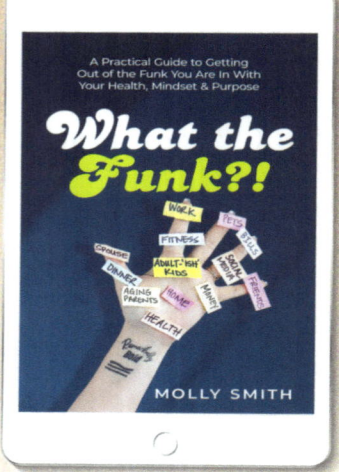

What the Funk?!
Molly Smith

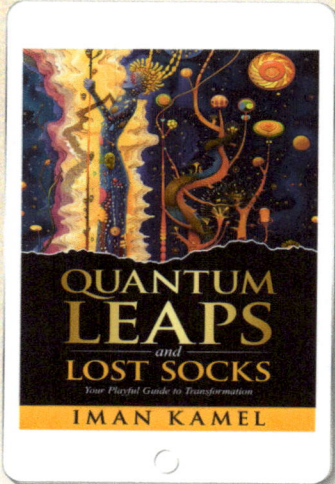

Quantum Leaps and Lost Socks
Iman Kamel

Radiate: Unleash Your Inner Light
Raeyan Goff

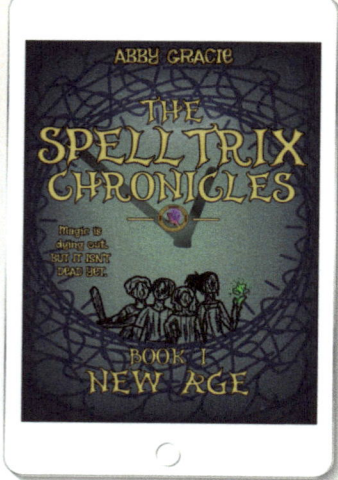

The Spelltrix Chronicles - Book 1 -
New Age - Abby Gracie

As if By Magic -
Lucy Kobier

SHE RISES
STUDIOS

UNLEASH YOUR STORY
BECOME A PUBLISHED AUTHOR!

Have you ever dreamed of sharing your wisdom, experience, or passion with the world? **Now is your time!**

Publishing a book isn't just about writing—it's about **establishing your authority, inspiring others, and creating a lasting legacy.** Plus, with the **$138.5 billion book industry** booming, there's never been a better moment to step into the spotlight.

At **SRS Publishing**, we don't just publish books—we **elevate voices, empower authors, and create change-makers.** Our mission is to help women break barriers, amplify their stories, and thrive in the publishing world. Whether you're an entrepreneur, thought leader, or storyteller at heart, **we're here to guide you every step of the way.**

JOIN THE FASTEST-GROWING PUBLISHING HOUSE FOR WOMEN IN THE USA.

READY TO TURN YOUR DREAM INTO REALITY?

 www.SheRisesStudios.com | contact@sherisesstudios.com

ANJALI
SUD

Elevating Video Creativity Through Vimeo's App Innovation

Anjali Sud has redefined the digital video landscape through her leadership at Vimeo, transforming it from a niche platform into a powerful tool for content creators, businesses, and filmmakers. As CEO, she spearheaded Vimeo's shift toward a creator-first ecosystem, leveraging mobile technology to make high-quality video production, editing, and distribution more accessible. Under her guidance, Vimeo evolved from a traditional video-sharing site into an advanced platform that empowers users to create, collaborate, and monetize content through cutting-edge app-driven solutions.

In an era where video consumption dominates digital engagement, Sud recognized the need for an alternative to ad-driven platforms like YouTube. Instead of competing for views and ad revenue, she focused Vimeo's strategy on providing professional-grade tools that enable creators to craft high-quality content without the limitations of intrusive advertising. This vision aligned perfectly with the rise of mobile content creation, where apps play a crucial role in streamlining the video production process. By prioritizing app-based innovation, Sud ensured that Vimeo remained at the forefront of the creative economy, catering to a diverse range of users—from independent artists to large-scale enterprises.

Vimeo's mobile app became a cornerstone of this transformation, offering an intuitive interface for shooting, editing, and sharing videos on the go. Recognizing that modern creators require flexibility, Sud led initiatives to integrate AI-powered editing, cloud storage, and collaboration tools directly within the app. These features allowed users to produce polished, professional-grade content without the need for expensive software or desktop-based workflows. The ability to edit and publish directly from a mobile device revolutionized how creators approached video production, making high-quality storytelling more accessible than ever.

Beyond individual creators, Vimeo's mobile innovations extended to businesses and enterprises, offering solutions for marketing, live streaming, and internal communications. The app's seamless integration with other digital platforms enabled brands to leverage video content for customer engagement, employee training, and virtual events. By expanding Vimeo's capabilities beyond traditional video hosting, Sud positioned the platform as an essential tool for digital-first businesses looking to harness the power of video storytelling.

A key aspect of Vimeo's growth under Sud was its emphasis on community and education. The platform introduced mobile-first tutorials, workshops, and interactive learning resources, helping users refine their skills and maximize the potential of video content. By combining technology with education, Vimeo became more than just a hosting service—it evolved into a creative hub where users could continuously enhance their craft.

Sud's leadership also emphasized inclusivity and diversity in digital storytelling. Through app-driven accessibility features, such as automated captioning and multi-language support, Vimeo ensured that content reached wider audiences, making it a valuable tool for global creators. By leveraging the power of mobile innovation, she democratized video production, giving independent filmmakers, educators, and small businesses the same high-quality tools previously reserved for major studios.

Anjali Sud's impact on the video industry is a testament to the transformative power of app-driven creativity. By prioritizing mobile technology, she positioned Vimeo as a leading platform for content creators, ensuring that high-quality video production is no longer confined to professionals with expensive resources. As mobile innovation continues to evolve, her vision for Vimeo remains a blueprint for how digital platforms can empower creators, redefine storytelling, and shape the future of video in an increasingly app-driven world.

NETWORKING WITH PURPOSE:

Leveraging Your Talents to Build Meaningful Connections

By Michele Gunn

Networking is defined as *"the action or process of interacting with others to exchange information and develop professional or social contacts."* It can and should be done in person, but you also have the option to network virtually. A combination of both would be ideal to truly grow your network

Gone are the days of just meeting people and collecting business cards in the hopes of acquiring new clients. Networking today is about mutual growth and connection, truly building relationships. Remember that every person has unique talents that can enhance their networking success. Utilizing your unique talents will help you stand out in the crowd and discover how to create a positive, lasting impression.

Recognizing and Leveraging Your Talents for Networking

Knowing your strengths and how they can serve others is a key part of self-awareness. Your natural abilities can make networking easier. Take inventory of your natural talents. Is communication, problem-solving, creativity, or recognizing how things are connected part of your innate talents? Leverage your talents to make a connection and build a relationship.

TIP: If you are not sure what talents you possess to leverage in networking, consider taking a strengths assessment (like CliftonStrengths) to identify your top talents. You can also invest in a coach to help you aim those talents.

Building Authentic Relationships, Not Just Contacts

Focus on quality over quantity in networking. It doesn't matter how many contacts you have if there are no relationships. People do business with people they know, like and trust. Those three attributes are based on a relationship, not collecting contact information. When you ask questions and listen, you can determine the best way to offer value to others first.

TIP: Practice active listening and find one way to support each new connection.

The Benefits of Networking for Personal and Professional Success

Networking has been traditionally viewed as an activity for professional growth. In reality, it also offers opportunities for personal growth. You can gain new perspectives, confidence, and lifelong friendships. Professional opportunities include career advancement, mentorship, collaborations and business growth. Ensure you are building relationships in alignment with integrity and service.

TIP: When meeting new people, keep an open mind to the kind of connection and relationship that could be built.

Practical Networking Strategies for Success

Be intentional in your networking strategies. Set goals such as who you want to meet and why. Keep in mind what you have to offer other people. Prepare a strong introduction by perfecting your elevator pitch with authenticity. Don't focus on the sale. Focus on the value you provide. Always follow up by sending a message, a connection request on LinkedIn, or set a future meeting. Give before you receive. Share resources, offer help, and create value. Asking questions will help you determine how to best be of value.

Strengthening Your Networking Skills

Practice sharing who you are in a compelling and authentic way. Attend small networking events to improve your confidence. Many times, virtual networking can be less intimidating. They may be a great place to build confidence.

TIP: Challenge yourself to connect with one new person each week.

Create a Networking Plan

Remember that networking isn't just about making connections. It's about cultivating relationships. Use your talents to connect with confidence and purpose. Plan on attending events and even joining a networking group. If you have not yet considered She Wins Women's Network, take a look. Membership includes in-person as well as virtual networking events. Check it out at www.michelegunn.com/houstonshewinswomensnetwork. When she wins, you win, we all win!

Connect With Michele

www.michelegunn.om
www.facebook.com/michele.jonasgunn
www.linkedin.com/in/michelegunn
www.instagram.com/michelegunn

The SHE RISES STUDIOS PODCAST

TUNE IN. RISE UP. THRIVE.

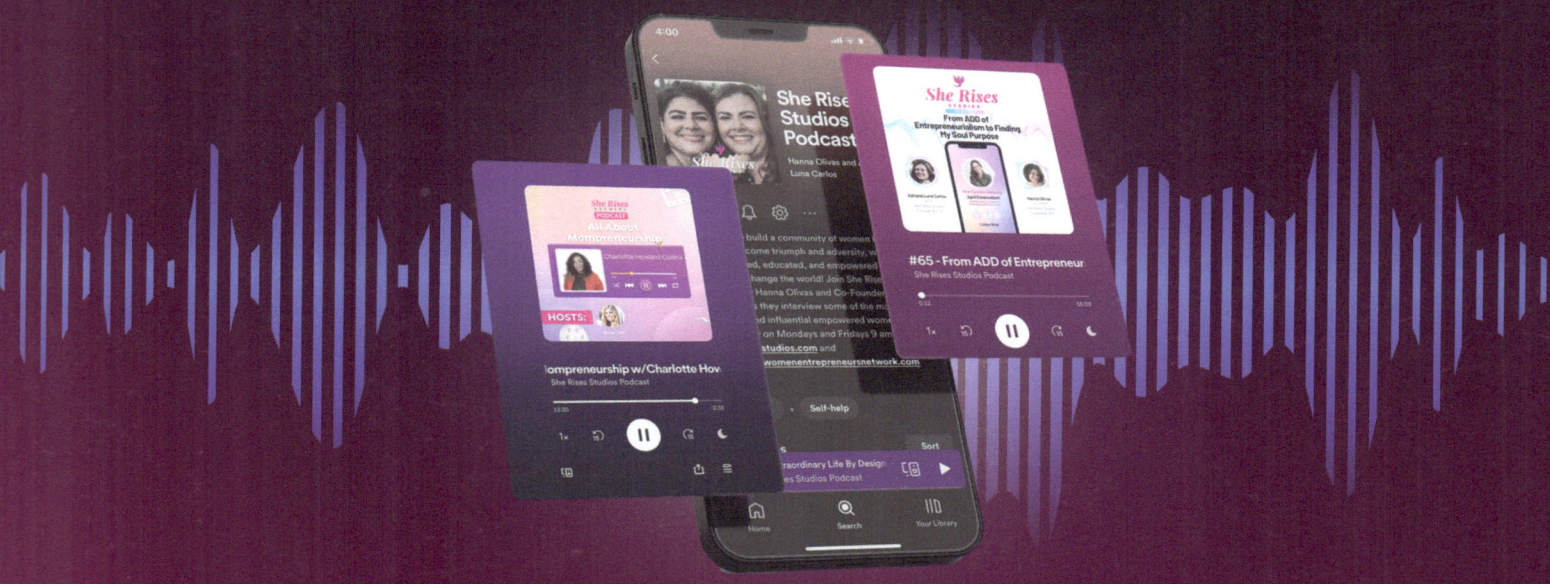

Looking for **real conversations** that inspire, empower, and ignite your potential? The **SRS Podcast** is where women like you come to **learn, grow, and rise!**

Join us for powerful **interviews with trailblazing entrepreneurs, thought leaders, and everyday women** who have turned obstacles into opportunities. Our episodes dive into:

➤ **Breaking through self-doubt** and stepping into confidence
➤ **Building a thriving business** with purpose and passion
➤ **Mastering work-life balance** without guilt
➤ **Leveling up your mindset, health, and career**
➤ **Finding your true purpose and living boldly**

Each episode is packed with **real stories, expert insights, and actionable strategies** to help you take your life to the next level. **This isn't just a podcast—it's your roadmap to success!**

SUBSCRIBE NOW AND START YOUR JOURNEY TO EMPOWERMENT!